The Blackest Guy with White Privilege

Words by H.M. Wiener
Pictures by Joseph Maslov

Dedication:

To Grandpapa.
Your constant love, support, and pride
for me helped me become that man I am
today. Thank you for accepting me as I am.

Gratitude:

I have to start by thanking my wife for
being so supportive of this journey. I would
also like to give a special thanks to Barney
for being my sounding board during the
whole process. Thank you to Joe for making
these experiences in my head come to life.

Thank you to those who looked at my idea
and disagreed with the notion that this was
stupid or unimportant; you know who you
are. And last but not least, thank you to all
the people who gave me the experience
I needed to make this book a reality; you
probably don't know who you are.

Hi! My name is Solomon, and let me tell you a little about myself.

Half my family is Black, and half my family is White.

Ethnically though, the White half of my family is Jewish and the Black half is African-American.

Growing up both in a multiracial and multiethnic household, I have had a pretty unique experience.

People have asked me what it's been like being half Black and half Jewish and it's been hard for me to answer them.

This is my way of sharing examples of my lived experiences with those who are curious.
This edition will focus on my racial mix.

By the end of this you will learn about my superpowers, my kryptonite, and everything in between. Enjoy!

I am White enough that.....

I feel like I stick out like a sore thumb if I am in an all Black neighborhood.

And I am Black enough that.....

I feel like I stick out like a sore thumb if I am in an all White neighborhood.

4

I am White enough that.....

I can have a White kid.

And I am Black enough that.....

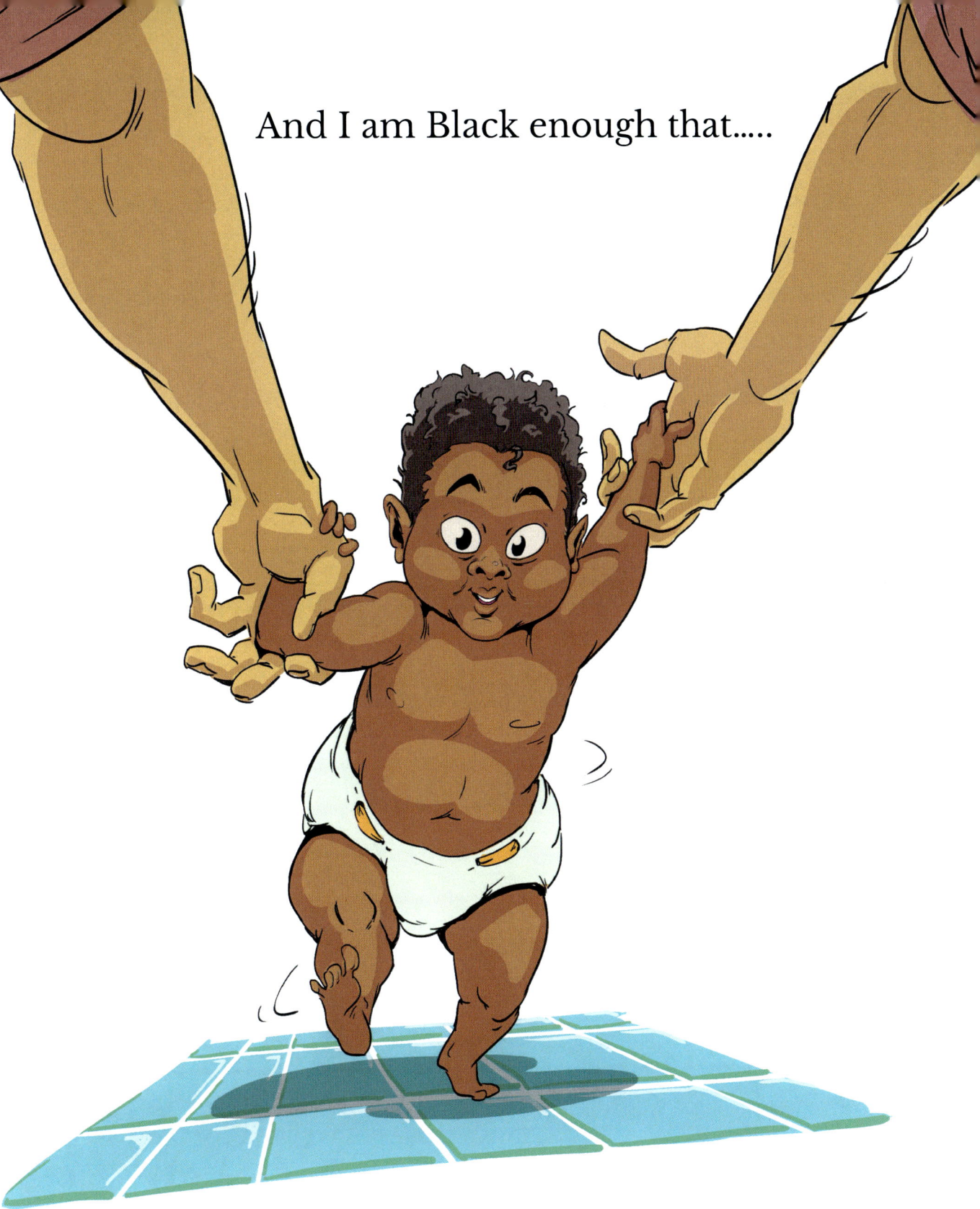

I can have a Black kid.

I am White enough that.....

I can get sunburned and need sunscreen.

And I am Black
enough that.....

I can get ashy
and need lotion.

8

I am White enough that.....

I have dressed up like Richard Simmons
for Halloween and no one batted an eye.

And I am Black enough that.....

I have dressed up like Barack Obama
for Halloween and no one batted an eye.

I am White enough that.....

I feel like a pretender when I am called Black.

13

I am White enough that.....

You see Solomon, black people say "SPECIFIC" like "PACIFIC".

It's something I wouldn't expect you to know.

Some Black family members who never felt quite Black enough finally get to feel blacker than someone in the family.

And I am Black enough that.....

I have always felt the need to hide
my hair's true form so that I can
fit in with Corporate America.

18

I am White enough that.....

I have never worried about
getting harassed by cops...

I am White enough that.....

You might say something to me that you normally wouldn't say to a Black person.

And I am Black enough that.....

White people get surprised
when they hear my name.

The Willaims Family Tree

I am
White enough that.....

Solomon

G. Uncle

G. Uncle

DAD

MOM

G. Dad

G. Mom

G.G Dad

G.G Aunt

G.G Uncle

G.G Mom

G.G.G Dad

G.G.G Mom

Maybe not-so-
Great-Gramps

Great x 5
Grandma

I have a direct ancestor who fought
in the US Civil War for the South.

23

And I am Black enough that.....

The sight of a confederate flag in public both scares me AND lets me know that I am not welcomed.

However,
I am Mixed enough that....

While I often get asked, "What are you?"
in some way, shape, or form,
I am proud of having such a diverse background.

Because I am Mixed enough that....

I get a unique view of multiple cultures that
I know millions of people do not get to have.

And I am Mixed enough that...

I know that deep down, we all feel like parts of ourselves are too much and other parts are too little, regardless of our

race, ethnicity, nationality,

sexual orientation, or physical appearance.

And I am
Mixed enough that...

I would not have it any other way.

About the Artist

Joseph Maslov is a story artist, illustrator, and art educator living in Portland OR.

He works in advertising and entertainment, including the Extra Credits History, Politics, and Mythology series.

He's excited by the specificity of deeply personal stories. Maybe he could draw your story.

JosephMaslov.com

About the Author

H.M. Wiener is originally from Georgia, but now lives in the great state of Washington. He works full time in the Tech-Industry, but he can't code to save his life. When not working, you can find him spending time with his wife and daughter, learning about the world via history, language, or flags, or thinking through his next passion project, like this one!

Made in the USA
Middletown, DE
23 December 2025

24934026R00020